A BEGINNER'S GUIDE TO BECOMING YOUR PARENTS

CHRISTOPHER GRILLO

ASSURE PRESS

Copyright © 2021 by Christopher Grillo

All Rights Reserved. No part of this book may be performed, recorded, used or reproduced in any manner whatsoever without the written consent of the author and the permission of the publisher except in the case of brief quotations embodied in critical articles and review.

ASSURE PRESS

An imprint of Assure Press Publishing & Consulting, LLC

www.assurepress.org

Publisher's Note: Assure Press books may be purchased for educational, business, or sales promotional use. For information please visit the website.

A Beginner's Guide to Becoming Your Parents/ Christopher Grillo— 1st ed.

ISBN-13: 978-1-954573-20-8
eISBN-13: 978-1-954573-21-5
Library of Congress Control Number: 2021930006

To my parents, of course, for whom this book is named.

To my wife, Victoria: the primary inspiration for these words, and most everything else I do in this life.

And to my newborn son, Luciano: I hope that someday you'll feel compelled to read my work and it teaches you something about yourself. If nothing else, perhaps you'll find this dedication worth showing off to friends.

I have my small necessities of honor in the same proportions as we have our great and enveloping love. You cannot have the one without the other.

— COLONEL RICHARD CANTWELL, *ACROSS THE RIVER AND INTO THE TREES*

PREFACE

Dear User,

Please read carefully through this instruction booklet before installing or operating your machine. The following instructions should prevent the risk of personal injury, damage to the machine, and/or collateral damage.

Please keep these documents in a safe place for later reference.

This operating manual has been written for several different machines, and some of the features mentioned here may not apply to your particular model.

CONTENTS

BOOK 1: HOW TO FALL IN LOVE
I: Love Yourself   3
A. Service & Troubleshooting   4
II: The Why   6
III: What You're Looking For   7
IV: The Doing   9
V: Talk to a Friend   10
A. REQUIRED TOOLS [NOT INCLUDED]   12
VI: First Dates & Making Conversation   13
B. REQUIRED TOOLS [NOT INCLUDED]   15
VII: The Test   16
VIII: Building Trust   17
IX: The First Fight   18
Considerations for Downed Removal   20
X: Have an Honest Discussion   21

BOOK 2: HOW TO PUT DOWN ROOTS
FIGURE A [The Exemplar]   27
FIGURE B [Reverse Engineering the Anecdote]   29
I. Get an Education   31
A. REQUIRED TOOLS [NOT INCLUDED]   34
II. Seek Employment   35
III. Financial Security   39
B. REQUIRED TOOLS [NOT INCLUDED]   42
IV. A Place to Lay Your Head   44
ii. A Friend's Place   46
iii. Your Own Place   47
iv. Owning Your Place   49
A. SERVICES & TROUBLESHOOTING   50
V: Become a Member of a Community   52
B. REQUIRED TOOLS [NOT INCLUDED]   54

BOOK 3: HOW TO LET GO OF ANGST
I. Understand your Angst 57
II. Trace the Source 59
III. Grieve 62
FIGURE A [Wind Song] 63
A. REQUIRED TOOLS [NOT INCLUDED] 65
IV. Manage 66
A. SERVICE & TROUBLESHOOTING 67
V. Spin It 69
B. SERVICE AND TROUBLESHOOTING 71
VI. When it Rears its Ugly Head 72

About the Author 75

A BEGINNER'S GUIDE TO BECOMING YOUR PARENTS

BOOK 1: HOW TO FALL IN LOVE

I: Love Yourself

First you must love yourself,
or at least pretend to,
even whilst your fist
encloses your own heart
so completely that no love
leaks,

not into the world,
and not

into the other rooms
of the body where it sleeps,

wakes,
works,
drinks,
sleeps,
repeats.

Should you feel some love
slip, squeeze tighter. This may hurt.
Check mirrors often to ensure
your grimace still resembles
a smile.

A. SERVICE & TROUBLESHOOTING

In Case of Saw Jam

1. It would be a day's work, clearing the fallen tree which told the tale of a storm whose self-loathing did not attend to collateral disorder. Back then I was convinced I'd be worth one less shit each day I did not restore curb appeal, but a man is most sure of himself in moments like these, having peeled off and wrung out clothes pressed wet in doubt, and dabbed the body dry of shame, all but that which sits in damp beads on the crust of his naked form.
2. I was not just optimistic. I was certain, and never more motivated than by the climb back to zero, one painstaking integer at a time. The only problem I foresaw were the small branches at the ends of the tree limbs, the fingertips of disaster, pinched between fence, spindle, and post, encroaching on the properties both west and south of my own. That is where I would start.
3. A borrowed chainsaw is of little use when your elbow deep in a mess of your own doing. It's not that I'd never been in the shit, but those were one bedroom, third and fourth floors, three hundred square feet, *could be taken care of with grab bag of hand tools* type places.
4. The first cut felt good, and me? I was all man. But the wood was live and green, and the mouth that formed from the two halves of trunk filled fast with chunks of damp pine like steel cut oats. I tried to withdrawal, but the tree bit hard, snapping down on the saw's bar and hanging on by the bottom teeth of the chain as I pulled. I stepped back, watched smoke tumble out from the motor in small circles and disappear in the sky. The saw,

stuck like Excalibur, a taunting reminder that I was unworthy.
5. What artistry was I to know of another man's tension screw, or the adjustment of bar bolts, or the angle of approach, or the touch of the trigger?
6. And so that day's work, which was to be spent cleaning the slate was wasted in tedium, coaxing tools into the roles they'd meant to serve, the burden of starting over made greater when negligence met disaster, and disaster met misestimation.
7. Since that, on any spring morning, you can find me set up on the driveway in genuflect, filing, a crisp air and a clean lawn, making damn good work of maintenance.

II: The Why

Decide why it is you want
to fall in love.

Decide,

despite having tried
and tried
and failed.

Man made for summit
a dozen times
before he heard
the voice of the mountain.

Lucky *a baker's dozen*,
as a determiner,
has transcended the days
when it meant a free loaf
of bread.

III: What You're Looking For

Consider what you're looking for.

Make a list. Frankenstein her
from all those failed expeditions:

short, dark, light eyes;
smart, but not smarter than you,
but just as smart (maybe);
likes what she likes,
and doesn't pretend to like
the New York Jets,
because even if she's a good liar,
eventually she'll break
and then, well...

Concede that you've no say in the matter, really.
Just hope that whatever *it* is,
the thing you cite when asked *why do you love me?* is made of the
same stuff that leans
ball players into fastballs.

She'll work to pry at each closed finger,
and open the fist that grips your heart
(which she believes it is still salvageable)
like the gradual peeling of a flower,

not a perennial,
but an intermittent,
until the day it becomes unclenched,
reaches full bloom.

They do not call it what it is then:
an infinite,
able to hold up to any frost,
but they should.

IV: The Doing

Meet someone.

The acting word
of much importance, here.

Meet,
not seek.

Let your heart guide you,
and tell you this new place is "threatening"

"menacing"
"ominous"
"etc."

Ignore said heart (the acting word,
ignore,
is of much importance here,
not so different than "trust")
for it is misguided, having been
strangled and starved of air
for so long.

V: Talk to a Friend

The heart will lead you,
among other places,
to a loud, crowded bar.

Many loud crowded bars.
Alone.
And with her.
With other hers.
And then, with her again.
And alone again.
Then, with a buddy:

At EJ Nevins, we drank brown liquor,
took smoke breaks out front,

stared across another New England in February's
shit stained,
half assed, snow plowed
street
at the Ulbrich Steel Factory.

It had to be the last one like it for miles and miles
and miles and miles…

And all of those rhetorical miles
could've stretched from anywhere.

We argued over the scene
and which flyover state
it was more characteristic of than ours,
(though neither of us had ever

been west of Philly).

If the moment were photographed
and lost for someone to find,
we wondered what hard day they might imagine
earned us those drinks and those smokes:

a machinist machining in one of the Dakotas,
a trooper trooping through Jackson Hole.
Anything really,
other than what was.

A. REQUIRED TOOLS [NOT INCLUDED]

Confidence

1. Do you remember how the old coach used to scoff at your taped cleats? *What is the purpose?* he'd say, not really asking. Of course, he was right and you were just gussying up, but at very least he understood superstition.
2. That substitute athletic trainer, though (probably a tennis player in his day), knew nothing. *A waste of tape,* he told you. *No real ankle support.*
3. He was right, too, but this was the quarterfinals, soon to be regarded as the worst you'd ever played.
4. I'm not saying that you couldn't block the Hand linebackers because your cleats weren't spatted, but I'm not not saying it either.

VI: First Dates & Making Conversation

But then, on other nights,
your heart will lead you here:

ask her

about herself,
her friends,
family,
long, longer, and longest
term goals.

She'll have to be judicious with words,
choosing and speaking them well
so that they are heard the first time
they are said.

The bar noise will visibly irritate you.

She'll touch your hand to tell
you *it's okay,* or *cut the shit*
(the two are interchangeable here).

You'll skip right to the heavy stuff,
realize you've said too much,

redact and mop up what's leaked,

the love oozing through the creases in command
that's loosened now around the heart.

Lean back in your seat.

Get your head out of there.

Touch each thumb to nose
to check that hands are eye level,

haven't tired or sank,
and can still defend.

B. REQUIRED TOOLS [NOT INCLUDED]

Class

1. So distant is what we conceive to be the things our lovers admire in us from what is actually admirable. To exist somewhere in this vast *between*, is to demonstrate true sophistication.
2. The trappings of new or prospective love are strange, and the tension on ties that fasten across two-top tables and train cars is strong. We are conditioned, rather than loosen or snip completely, to take measurements, replace with wire rope, something sturdier, that will hold up a while.
3. This is accomplished when the cheese cloth separating thought from speech, is bypassed and we act on the same impulse that made us cringe when it first flashed across our mind's eye, words in red-light district neon we could not help but read aloud.

VII: The Test

Check compatibility. I find it best
to use an always, sometimes, never, not applicable
survey system.

Never answer not applicable.

Always leave your name in the open-ended response box.

Ignore answers to all questions
except:

"does your partner know the very specific difference

between working on a dream,

and simply dreaming?"

VIII: Building Trust

If you have gotten to this point,
it is likely that you already trust her,

and if you do not,
you do not admit this,
but rather acquiesce

that should she feel compelled
to break sanctity, then that feeling is borne in her, part of
her DNA,

and any preemptive measure you might take,
that friends have taken and instructed you to take will be useless

(like when you met her 'friend' and squeezed
until the knuckles pressed together, and
you stared and waited for his face to break)

More than likely,
in fact,
these will prove themselves
counterproductive.

Instead, be a beacon of loyalty.
Let that mantra you share with the neighborhood boys,
that has been so misplaced in other factions of life, be put to
some good
damn
use.

IX: The First Fight

At first, you will be able to deal with conflict appropriately. You
will do this with relative ease
because where you are standing with her
is still very close to the place where
you stood alone.

Time is a double-edged sword, though,
because soon it will afford you the luxury
of forgetting what life was like without.

Then, there will be moments like these,
and you'll wish that someone would remind you that you were
born a have not,
and all current angst is simply a stage evolved
from former angst which was rooted in desperate longing
to have.

Psychologists assert the next few minutes
are a direct result of the adverse childhood
experiences you've collected,
and because your collection is stout,
you live in a constant place of fight or flight:

Allow your conscience the freedom to respond
from that fast deepening, receding,
revolting time when you were on your own.

(Should you choose to fight)
You are going to blow this.

(And should you choose to fly)
Winners never quit.

B. SERVICE & TROUBLESHOOTING

Considerations for Downed Removal

1. In assessing the size of the tree, however inadvertent its fall, you will find yourself standing, looking, laughing a little, surveying your rendered kingdom, which has fulfilled its tragic prophecy, and is now in ruins. In Rome, and Greece people stand in ancient buildings and tell stories of how folks lived before they burned. I think these monuments are poor criteria by which to judge. How is anyone to really know how another man lived?
2. Think of how easy it would be right now, to concede that this configuration of debris, the staked boundary of area where dead limbs have landed, will be the one to bear your remembrance. It is a decision often made frivolously, singing self-sacrifice over horns of surrender that are too loud to think through. But then there are moments where the horns fade in decrescendos drawn out long enough for other options to reveal themselves for weighing. Perhaps, this is a time for dusting off the file, for kneeling, for tedium, and sharpening.
3. You choose this alternative, not because you believe in yourself, but because you have sensed what others- bigger, stronger, and steadier- have not left to ruin, and so through simple, mathematical correlation, you see that rate of change and probability of goodness in you are near enough that you may, after all, be needed, or at the very least, utilized.

X: Have an Honest Discussion

(See Sec. VI, *First Dates and Making Conversations*)

i.

You have already, albeit accidently,
said more truth
than is needed up to this point.

That is not a bad thing
because since then, you've held some back,
only offered peaks through closet doors
you swore were bulk head,

but have since been replaced
with shutters, or perhaps
they had been letting light in the whole time.

It is possible that for this reason,
or innumerable other possibilities
for an equal amount of reasons,
that she loves you,
and because she is better than you,
she tells you.

You will be in bed when it happens,
not sleeping together,
but having just slept together.
It will be morning.
The sun will pour through the windows,
bounce off the dull green panelboard covering your bedroom walls,

and light the both of you up like test subjects,
each for the other to study.
All imperfection glorious.

Remember that room? At the place on Simpson Ave? You had
fun there.
Single, and thus singular, in your needs and desires
and so, you never bothered
to blind the eyes on the face of that house
because you liked the idea of a natural alarm,
and because, let's face it, you wouldn't know
where to get curtains if you had to.

You will laugh and say "thank you"
because you mean it.

Her spirit will collapse and you will kick yourself,
not because you lied by omission. That isn't it.
You will know your own love is implied
and so, your regret will be that you did not explain
what you actually meant when you
thanked her—

that the world expects us to love,
but makes no dispensations when the love is hard; that you
think she is brave,
and that you are grateful.

*This section has been amended
from a previous version,

    not because you were unsure,

but simply because engagement rings

    are expensive (see Book 2, Sec. V)
    and timing is a skill

        to be mastered with age. More vital,
        coming to terms with the idea

            that when it comes to gestures,
            our conception of grand

                is far from what is verifiable.
                Grand happens,

                    where she happens,
                    and where you and
                    she happen together,

            because love is grand,
            and all this just over analysis

        of advice meant to be read plainly:
        just ask. Do it with a command

    using a period, but that implies inquiry,
    because that is more your style.

Marry me.

BOOK 2: HOW TO PUT DOWN ROOTS

FIGURE A [THE EXEMPLAR]

My old man gets up
(but does not wake)
at 3:30
every morning.
He stretches through
one of 4 pocket t-shirts he owns,

all the same brand—
tough enough not to tear
when his climb boots slip
and he hugs a telephone pole.

He stumbles downstairs
and reheats yesterday's coffee
in a sauce pan,
adding heavy cream and stirring
at a rate of 30 full clockwise
rotations per minute.

I know this because I have watched
having been stirred myself
by the sound of kitchen hardware
bumping in its hurry
out of the cupboard
like rush hour commuters
through subway doors.

The first time I heard him,
I unsheathed the pine tarred
Louisville Slugger
from under my bed,

tiptoed to the stairs' first landing,
and peaked through spindles
only to find the old man
stirring and counting
with a patience that is only demonstrated
by someone who'd been in REM
just 20 minutes prior.

Before then, I could not have said,
with any degree of certainty,
what time dad left for work.
I knew he'd be gone before I woke,
and home when I arrived back from school,
dozed on the couch,
still wearing shoes,
Mike Francesca chastising Met fans
over the radio,
a pound of beef
thawing on the kitchen counter.

FIGURE B [Reverse Engineering the Anecdote]

When I was a kid, I assumed
my father's pocket t-shirts were a bad
style choice. Turns out
they had practical application,

like tools he kept upstairs
in his and my mom's bedroom,
instead of on a hook in the garage,
because he knew he would need one
as soon as he woke up.

Each was faded or bleach stained
or both, and fit snug across his torso
and loose in the arms,
per the dimensions of someone

who earned muscle in the world
and not the gym.
And he always had something stuffed
in the breast pocket. Usually a pen,
the outline of some change,

                              and what were
certainty the last few
sticks from a pack of big red,
but sometimes something ridiculous
that the pocket was ill-equipped
to hold:

a tape measurer
that nearly tore the top seams

of the pouch,
or a once folded newspaper,

two thirds
flopping opposite the direction he moved.
All of this, I thought, made him look
like a bad ass, and so on the mornings
his sauce pot coffee procedure woke me,

I'd run down the hall to peep
what color he wore,
and the corresponding pant choice,

and I'd mimic the outfit with the closest thing I had. Then, I'd
get downstairs and he'd ask

what I was doing up and ten other unrelated questions. Finally,
he'd notice our corresponding
outfits, make a passing dad joke,
like *Nice shirt, ace! Where'd ya get it!*
I am unsure if he knew,
or if he genuinely believed it coincidence.
Either way, I've never told him
that it wasn't.

I. Get an Education

Read often and for pleasure.
Play outside in lieu of T.V.
and gaming. Cease
only when breadth of vocabulary
overshadows

inherent intelligence,
creating illusion of above average
intellect, or

you become cool—
whichever happens first.

Table it.
The reading and imagining.

Become social and self-conscious,
trimming bushy eyebrows into pencil lines,
and stealing Mom's cover up
because proactive
only ever worked for Mandy Moore.

                              Explore outside
the range
of the moral compass
given to you in catechism
from Miss Hackett,
who was so mean,
only the exact opposite
of what she said could have been Godly.

Pick fights. Lose some.
Dip Sharpie Marker into pool
of creativity you've been suppressing
for your masterpiece:
a bust of Principal Hercsher
as decorated Nazi SS on the bathroom stall
partition in B hall.

Intercept report cards in the mail.
Pay tech savvy friends to scan
and change grades. Get caught
and assert to parents
that you are just
not
smart.

Find sport, a place where angst
is useful, and consequently,
a reason to strive for B's.

Strike a deal with Ms. August
in order to pass statistics.
Despite better judgment,
apply to college. Take comfort
in the fact that there are sports there,
and girls,
and parties.

Find a new brand of angst
when Professor Foster
laughs at your independent
study proposal to explore
sport as narrative.

You will infer
that he has never
been punched in the face before,

otherwise
he would not be laughing.
Though tempted,
you cannot act,

but must quell (see Book 3, sec. IV).
Years later,
speak of scare moments
of productive regret,
and tell this story.

A. REQUIRED TOOLS [NOT INCLUDED]

Strength

1. In a warm state in February, a tired man dozes body sinking in bed of sand. His back will pay for this come morning. He stirs when college girls begin to cluster, watches them stand waist high in blue water, admiring the bodies of boys they've watched grow from freshman into near-men.
2. The fellas know it, too and so they clench their stomachs between football throws. They cuss loud so that the girls in the water can feel their edges.
3. Time passes. A strange, new, yard game emerges, its purpose indiscernible to the man. There's a beer run, and the car comes back plus one: a black kid in short floral trunks wears a snake like a winter scarf. There is a chicken fight, and after a while, some barking and nearly a real one over a beach chair, the tired man thinks.
4. It is at this, that he perks, one-part intrigue, one-part concern for his own tribe: the tired woman sleeping next to him who he is proud has not seen enough fighting to distinguish chicken from fisticuffs by the sound each makes.
5. The squabble fizzles off and he is again in conflict, relieved that the status quo has been returned, that boys are still boys, and men, men, and that strength is negated when there is nothing to move or to bear, but a bit disappointed that he was deprived the chance to show them this, or better yet, to find these were truths they'd already come to know.

II. Seek Employment

Your old man
takes odd overtime hours
in weather that chaps skin
beyond the point of moisturizing replenishment.
He does this, so that he can slip you crisp twenties when he
drops you at the Showcase Cinema
on Fridays.

If this sounds familiar,
than it is likely
that on your 16th birthday,
with hands hard and swollen like catcher's mitts,
he escorts you through the door
of the local meat market,
and asks owner and proprietor,
Bob Shea, if he hires high school kids.

Bobby wonders if you clean up
after yourself at home. He knows your mother,
and that you likely don't clean,
but that you *can* clean,
and that you will.

Bobby knows you will
because he also knows
your father, and trusts
that you have come to understand
that if *work was meant to be fun they'd call it play.*

Your job is mostly

the sterilization of machinery
where various parts
of various animals
are manipulated in shape or consistency

such that sausage appears
the way sausage is *supposed* to,
and not as a lug of pork butt chunks
and fennel.

Pay attention
and recognize the irony in this,
and years later, you will find
that this is the nature of every profession
across every industry.

Maintain this job beyond high school,
because it is flexible
and because the beer fridge
does not fill itself.

Soon, you notice the faces
of parents whose kids
you grew up with
sadden when you turn
to wrap their minute steaks
because they think you've resigned
to this life indefinitely.

Graduate
to assistant meat cutter,
which is lucrative around the holidays,
and worth the way your relationship
with chicken is forever changed,

and even worth it when classmates
home for winter break,
the ones whose parents
cast the judgey eyes,
are sent down to the store
to pick up the Christmas roast.

Years later, settle into the job you landed
with the degree you earned
reading Victorian Poetry in between
grinds of boneless Chuck scraps.
The uniform will be different,
and most days, there is less blood,

but there are still occupational hazards,
like the bill you pay each month
for the education you needed
just to have sat at the table
with other industry men.

Find that what you do
with your life versus what you don't do
almost always nets zero,
and that prospering
lies in the *how*
and the *why*.

Hear of the meat market's closing,
and of Bob Shea's declining health.
Reckon that everything you tell young kids
about *finding your calling*
can be traced back to the store,
and hate yourself for being too busy
to stop by on Christmas Eve

and shoot whiskey with everyone
while Bobby ties the last Prime Rib of the shift.

III. Financial Security

Growing up, learn quickly
the difference between financial
security & financial freedom,

which manifest themselves
in the exact way monikers
suggest. Your childhood

is secure. Your appetite, warmth,
and ability to learn and play,
fiercely kept within acreage
slightly less bound

than that of your parents.
They are your keepers,
keeping good
on a promise
made to one another

to conduct the survey themselves,
marking terrestrial position of points
around your life
wider,
higher,
and deeper
than what they knew.

They do not do so
frivolously, though,
and on the day

the borders are raised,
they disregard
recommendations of parents
they know
that *all you will need is ranch rail*

and employ a hinge-joint
at double the fence height for post
depth, despite code being half that.

Security, then, as a descriptor
in the context of your coming
of age, is different from *freedom,*
and is a misnomer.
The people who *secure*
your *freedom,*
namely your parents,
are themselves indentured
to the work of keeping
those borders in place.

Grow up in the same town,
and go to the same schools
as the McGuire kids.

Your dad's even work the same shifts,
but Aaron and James see
Disney the summer
before fifth grade,

while you learn
and master the cross cut
pattern of the lawn,
now that you're tall enough

to reach the handles on the walk behind
mower, and strong enough
to squeeze the clutch.

Soon, Mr. and Mrs. McGuire divorce.
This happens after Aaron and James realize
their parents don't argue
like everyone else's,
but before either
boy has aged past questions like
why did we have to move?

B. REQUIRED TOOLS [NOT INCLUDED]

Honor

1. It will be your father who first pays you the compliment, but this will be years after he's explained the weight of it. In the meantime, say you were chasing it, but know that this is not true.
2. Why do believers ask what Jesus would do? Because they are aware of the prospect of heaven in the same way they are aware that they are breathing, and so their lives only allow reflection on what this means in few dark, quiet places—places where suffocation seems imminent: right before sleep, or in confessional booths.
3. Hear it said of your freshman football coach who is forced to resign after hosting a party for his son, the senior quarter back. Do not let this confuse you. Despite whispered judgements of moms in grocery lines about town, the standard your old man set all those years ago, does not lower. You know the coach, and that he lives to bridge the valleys that over protective parents dig between boys, and the game he believes forged the best parts of him.
4. Years later, think about the violence with which you treated the man across the ball, get meta while you wait in office lobbies sizing up other job applicants through small talk, and learning enough to hate them.
5. Protect the people who deserve protection, and love, and gratitude and if in dark, quiet places your mind is not honorable, or in bars your tongue disloyal, fear not. Whispering judgements in grocery store lines about town are only valid if concerned with action or inaction

when action is what is needed. Not talk (never talk), or the places a tired mind wanders just before sleep.
6. At the end of the day, it does not matter if you were captain of the team, or what school you went to, or how much money you made. The highest compliment someone could ever pay you is to say you are a good man.

IV. A Place to Lay Your Head

i. Your First Place

should be seedy,
and in those maiden months,
there may even be a murder on the third floor,

or at the very least,
attempted.

Take note of faded white
numbers centered in each parking space

marking tenant territory.
Use these to assign
laundry room faces

with vehicles:
a valuable tool in the construction
of preconceived notions.

A few weeks later,
the shock wears off,
and the cars cease to speak
to the culpability

of owners, and return
to what they've always been:

steel tombs left behind each night
to cool and creak

in plots we work all our lives
to overpay for,
until the next domestic squabble.

ii. A Friend's Place

Graduate to a friend's rental property,
which is a hand shake deal,
but then that first winter
the water heater shits the bed.

This is where you live
around the time you meet the girl
you will ask to be your wife,

the same house with the panel boarded
bedroom, (see book 1. sec V)
and where she first sees what you can be,
trying to act grown,

first with your dad's Channel Locks, fumbling
for Teflon tape while you work to patch
the leak. Then, pawning a takeout

meal as your own cooking,
forgetting her lactose intolerance,
but remembering a handwritten note
and to stop at Cumbies
for some flowers.

Going forward,
these will not cut it,
but for now, you're showing promise.

III. Your Own Place

Soon, you reach the age
where it is no longer appropriate
to have roommates. Spend the summer

with your parents who you love,
but who are the least appropriate
kind of roommates.
Agree to a year lease

on the third floor
of a hot pink multi-family.
The girl likes it, though,

and spends a few nights
a week with you there,
cooking, laughing,

and playing house.
In the mornings,
you walk down
to the coffee shop on the corner.

There is a sign there
discouraging the use

of electronic devices.
Much of the neighborhood
wastes the day here
reading and writing in large,

leather bound journals,

forgetting they are not in Paris
in the 20's.
Order a macchiato,

because though you've never had one,
this seems like the right place to get one.
It is served
as a shot of frothed espresso

and fails to shake the weight
from your eyelids.
On mornings she does not wake with you,
revert back to gas station coffee.
The Shell on the corner

has a nice selection
of Green Mountain.
You see bartenders

from Contoi's there,
the dive on the corner,
where the owner
threatens you because of your backwards hat.

Turn it around and finish your beer.
Embrace the paradox and the fact
that this is not your place
any more than the coffee shop.

iv. Owning Your Place

The first days of homeownership
are like inheriting a chainsaw,
or trying to make sense of someone else's
story. You can hear

the it's heartbeat.
You may even feel the pulse
of it, but it cannot be seen.
At least not yet.

On day one, pull chicken wire fence
from the yard that had been there so long
it had become rooted. Part of this fence
is attached to a telephone pole
sans telephone wires, which serves
as the counterpart to the house in
a clothes' line pulley system
that ran on the least sensible plane,
a corner bishop's path,
when a rook's was available.

A. SERVICES & TROUBLESHOOTING

Preemptive Overgrowth Management

1. We'd never met him, the former owner, Vinny, only ever heard stories from Carlo and Josephine, the Italians next door: how he set an old toilet on the curb weeks before bulk pickup and after he'd already lost the house.
2. Carlo gave more context one day while I was weed whacking around the mailbox (or trying to). They had been golf buddies before Vinny's divorce. Having caught wind of neighborhood complaints concerning the roadside commode, ol' Vinny took a ride over, and planted a big, beautiful bouquet at the center of the pot.
3. I couldn't help but like him a bit for acting on his resentment, and all at the same time, hate him for the mess he'd left me.
4. Swing your axe. Wield the steel bodied set of electric hedge clippers that you inherited from your granddad, like a legacy sword. Ever since you filed the teeth of its blade, it has become the subject of many *they don't make 'em like they used to*'s.
5. Despite this, a year in, with Vinny a relic of a time when men let their little disappointments fester and grow, you are still fighting in dark corners of the yard. Because that is exactly what they are: weeds and vines and thorns, the little fingers of demons, our disappointments, which given free reign will spread and grow and tie down whole structures like those rooted in the ground, pulled taught over the shed's roof, and latched to tree limbs above.

6. All life, then, and all living, or purposeful living is the maintenance of a tidy yard, the clipping of those little monster finger nails, lest all your joy lie in the sad irrigation of flowers by toilet water.

V: Become a Member of a Community

Throughout the home buying process,
your agent will stress the importance
of location as a determinant
for value. From this, infer
that your own location is prime,

a stone's throw from the River House Tavern,
which is a proper dive
in that it doesn't even pretend
to serve food. In this way, it is like the bar

where you and the girl had your first date,
the first demonstration
of your fluid relationship with time
the last one that was endearing to her,

but resoundingly not
that bar.

And you are not that guy anymore,
which is why she agrees to pick
you up there at the end of the night.

As you have come home again,
despite Thomas Wolfe's cautionary
tale, it is important to meet old friends
after long, hot days carting rubbish

from the driveway turnaround
where the former owner of your new home
piled it, to its rightful place

at the mouth of woods
in the backyard. One night,

you're introduced to a jack of all trades
laborer with a braided pony tail named Gene.
Unprompted, he explains that he grows
his hair out to donate. You didn't think
anything of it, you say, but you're oddly
disarmed.

Get to talking with him,
tell him of your septic system woes:
a compromised distribution box,
which is technical language used to describe
the potential for a literal shit storm
in the house. Gene happens to be
in the business of under cutting septic engineers.

He makes light of your problem,
and agrees to look at it for nothing.
Now, that you know that Gene
is not a pony tail guy, but rather, a guy
that happens to have a pony tail,

and because this is happening over beer
and you're both dirty and tired and a little drunk,
you can trust him.
Realize this
is why people move here,
and not, as they lie, for the schools.

B. REQUIRED TOOLS [NOT INCLUDED]

Sacrifice

1. To be *good,* one would have met other prerequisite criteria.
2. The eulogizer spoke fondly of the dead man on the rounds he drank which outweighed those he bought.
3. It is with the same reverence that high school kids, shielding their manhoods in gang showers, speak of the hustlers and playboys whom they never aspire to be.

BOOK 3: HOW TO LET GO OF ANGST

I. Understand your Angst

Whenever I merge onto a highway
it begins to rain
harder,

which necessitates the presumption
that it is always
raining. Or perhaps

it appears to be raining
harder
because I am driving
faster. This is what

it is
to live
with great angst:

to be going somewhere,
or to live with want
to go somewhere,

and suddenly,
to find yourself
stuck

behind something
big:

a semi
and its wash,
which is more frightening than it should be,

and creates a sense of danger
that does not exist in other lanes

beyond the spray radius of that wash. You know this,
and it pisses you off,
but you're not sure, because
despite your best efforts,
you cannot see to change lanes safely.

II. Trace the Source

At your peak,
you exist in attic crawl space,
eye each step you take

over insulation,
footing the strong intersection
of joists, and occasionally

risking a tightrope walk
along cross beams.

Eventually, you will fall.
It will feel like slipping,
and you will crash though many floors
landing, ultimately,
dust and debris covered,

at the ground level
before you ever find out
the truth: that you were pushed.

But by whom? is the wrong question.
Never are people solely to blame,
but unchallenged belief,

lack of perspective,
and weak conviction.

These are a Molotov cocktail,
and the human form, the bottle.

Let us be clear:
this description
is not to be cast in judgement

of others. It is nuclear ash
cloud covering,
ominous to you

and your perpetrators
in equal parts.
It describes you,
and you are its cause,
waving your spear mad
and menacing,
whilst they flash their shields,
egging you on. It will take much doing
before you are able to see yourself

and where on the narrative arc
you stood,
when you began to fall.

Here is how that story goes:
there is the singularity,
which maddens you blind.
You are beside yourself.

Time passes. Too much
to hate in the same way
you first did,

but not enough to heal
either. Then there is a welcoming face.
It smiles as it reaffirms you.

Hate like mine that smiles,
and does not scream,
is logical, you think.

So, you listen,
and devour,
and share in this meal with others
whom you call "comrade."

You must stand beside
them now, defend
and fight for them,
because you are loyal,
and honorable.

Soon you are no longer driven
by what you hated,
and the singularity
is a distant,
fading,

black and white memory.
Still, you cite it,
but it is just something
you say (no real sin)
to rationalize the things you do
(cause for current and ultimate judgement).

III. Grieve

Allow yourself to feel deep sorrow
over the things that were promised to you
or that you promised yourself, which were lost
or which you stepped over
unknowingly:

the grades you could have gotten;
the debt you could have avoided;
the girl(s) you could have been with
if only you'd been less
yourself. This is a time

to lament, which is another word
for grieve, but stronger
in that it contains two syllables
and connotes an unprecedented

vainness
in its focus on
"I."

I didn't have any guidance.
I am misunderstood.
I didn't start it
I don't deserve to be in this cell

I can't afford this
I contribute to society, why
are you punishing *me,*

I

FIGURE A [Wind Song]

The wind does not whisper. It is not so passive
and need not worry if shit talk
is overheard. It does not howl either,

since howling is meant for staking claim,
so, for the wind to howl,
would be ceaseless.
When the wind forces itself

through cracked and hollow tree limbs
that hover above my drive in October,
it merely blows
in a way characteristic of.

The only other human descriptor
that is apt to describe
as I hear,
is to say
it wails—

in mourning.
Not quite up to Catholic widow standards,
but enough to notice,
to become central thesis

in the day's small talk,
about scales of bark,
and other small digits,
that will need raking,
and dragging to the place

where brush breaks down and decays
behind the shed.

Enough already!
I scowl across the early hour,
but am discouraged

because the wind is faceless.
Quit your babbling!
I realize I am asking too much of him,
and though this is only heartache,

it feels like much more right now.
We all know that
because we all have known that,

and when the ball point hammer drops
dead center on the wind's porcelain heart,
which is always the way for men like us,
what then?
The whole of that big dead oak, like a knife
through the roof of the master bedroom?

It is a sad and beautiful truth of nature,
that only you
could be responsible for this.

A. REQUIRED TOOLS [NOT INCLUDED]

Integrity`

1. There was much that was overlaid, veneered, painted, and cased in facade. I did this, knowing it would last but the first big storm. I hadn't the time or the resources, and I told myself *next year*.
2. Then, it was next year, and there was less time, no money, and the storm season came early. And so, I masked over the masking, and vowed again.
3. This is how men live: without the courage to throw themselves from moving trains, without the strength to pull through the centrifugal force of spinning wheels, until they are at penultimate rest, or that eve less dignified, final stillness, stuck entangled in spokes.
4. So, I started with the demolition, a messy job, and standing amongst the rubble I knew the modern age did not allow for the leaf fires of simpler times. I'd have to call a guy, someone to do it the slow way, which is the right way, so that decomposition does not happen at the expense of the surrounding world.
5. Then came the building, both tedious and exhaustive in its demand for precision and force, precision and force, something like a passionate dance. I did this and I knew no one would be the wiser, and still I smiled because I did not care.

IV. Manage

You will find it is best to manage your angst
in one of 4 ways:

i. Fall in Love
(see Book 1)

ii. Drink

though this lacks efficiency
in that it requires subsidiary management tactics
or else you may squander love or create more angst
as a consequence of the drinking,
which, ironically was meant as a tool for angst management
in the first place.

iii. Identify A Primal Act

Something that gives you proper
reason to be tired at the end of the day,
not the illusion of fatigue you mind creates
through the expenditure of acting "professionally"
from 9am to 5pm.

iv. Write

Though this is not recommended if you
    a. do not write well, or
    b. do not write well and are frustrated
       by the lack of wellness in your writing
         which, in this scenario, will act much in the same way
         as drinking, or more likely, cause you to drink.

A. SERVICE & TROUBLESHOOTING

Caring for your Machine

1. The beauty of a working tool, is in not knowing why and how it is working. That is a job for guys like Al Brazil, lawnmower man, who sold me a shiny red Cub Cadet for $400. Then, one day, the lever that lowers the blade snapped, the deck stuck indefinitely at the lowest setting. I spent hours staring at the broken pieces trying to analyze their intended configuration, but ultimately called Al.
2. *Yeah, this is not what it's supposed to look like,* he said from his back aside the tractor. I swear I could hear his old bones whimper.
3. A few weeks later, the drive shaft broke free of the wheel that guides the mower. I am not actually certain it was the drive shaft, or if mowers even have drive shafts, but I had heard this term before, and what had broken, a steel arm that ran from the steering wheel to the front, left wheel, seemed like something that could, and logically should, be called a drive shaft.
4. I started off determined, until I found that the receiving end of the steering wheel arm was a ball bearing, and that the end of the arm itself was outfitted with a little spoon shape. It was obvious to me that these two pieces had been married, but still unclear how. Maybe a weld or some factory tool, that certainly Al Brazil had lying around at the shop, but fuck that. I wanted to cut my goddamn grass. It was dark by the time I had finished.
5. Drilling through the scoopy end of the steering wheel arm went quickly, believe it or not, but finding a screw,

or bolt, or token piece of galvanized steel thin enough to fit the hole and rigid enough to withstand the rough terrain of the yard, and the many sharp turns I'd make to avoid its impediments, took hours. I settled on a ½ inch bolt, and since I had no nut to lock it down, I summoned what stubborn desire for lawn care I had left, and using a pair of channel locks bent the bolt into a J.
6. So far it has held and I have realized that this is the way all yards are kept tidy. We use what is at our disposal to maintain the tools we need to do our job a little better, and that is all we can do.

V. Spin It

(See Book 2, Sec. II., Sub-sec. i., Lines 43-56)

That,
and more.

You will learn how to hustle:
first, in the job you work laying brick
during grad school,

not because you care deeply
if the Kaufman's 5000 dollar,
commissioned retaining wall
is both sturdy *and* aesthetically pleasing,
or that you've safely removed
all of the original concrete
from the Birdwhistle's diving board
base (3 feet deep. All rock)
so that the new blue stone deck
and subsequent pool coping
sits flush,

balls on by the level's bubble,

but because Doug, the foreman,
gave you some shit one day
about sitting in the AC when he needed you,
though you were under the impression
he was just running back
for his tools
(it's so like Doug to find more work when the job is done).

The insinuation will silence you,
as you boil in anger and then over,
dripping steadily and unpleasantly
because the humidity of August
in New England is the stuff of demons.

Doug will hit a Dunkin for a Coolatta
because, as he has expressed, brain freeze
cools him. He will ask if you would like one
and when you decline, he will take it
as personal insult, just as you had,

which is likely why you started riffing
back and forth in the first place.
You are of like minds, but then you had dated
his daughter years prior and it didn't end well,

but that is no matter. The next day,
and every day after,
you will work,
and work,
and carry,
and schlep,
and learn,

until you are working on Doug's crew
at his request.

B. SERVICE AND TROUBLESHOOTING

Upkeep

1. The more dimension you are able to amass between yourself and your last disaster the stronger your immunity will become to catalysts of ruin. This is sometimes called *restraint* but I like to think of it as *resistance,* less about will and so much more concerned with speed of trajectory.
2. You have found that open field encourages directness, that the luxury to side tract yourself sans consequence, is always overshadowed by your instinct which pulls you along a straight line, no give on the reel.
3. Say it again. Demand honesty of yourself: this has nothing to do with will power and everything to do with what you know of travel efficiency between two points. The only difference between good and bad, is the momentum you build. Both play in the same space, but carrying a full head of steam, you've always delivered more blows than you've taken

VI. When it Rears its Ugly Head

and it will
as fuel,
both to power your ambition
through the walls
the world (you are convinced)
has built to hold *you* back

and to spark the flame
that burns that life to the ground.

This is where it is important
to be frank with yourself.
Easier said,
and done through vehement
contention that the idea
of living without regret

is bullshit,
and is cowardly,
and reserved for the fortunate
who are afforded a life
free

of looking themselves in the mirror
and hating what they see
because they've been carried

over fissures that stop folks
like you and me,
cold.

Be grateful for this. It will serve you well,
though it does not seem so
now that you are at that edge,
looking out over the fall
and into the mirror,
and back at the fall,
and realizing this could have been avoided.

But I promise you it will,
and what's more, it will give the people
whom love you unconditionally,
but whom at any time can opt out
of unconditionality,
unlike parents, siblings,
and buddies,
a reason to stay:

This is who he is,
they'll say
and any consequence he faces
will be nothing compared to the size of the stones
he has already cast upon himself.

If you play your cards,
and you are, at heart, good and true,
this is what she will say

But she will not be there at all
if you do not first
let her chink the armor,
let her see you stumble over words
before her. Let her see you
struggle. Let her see you
cry.

Let her see you.

ABOUT THE AUTHOR

Christopher Grillo has published fiction and poetry in various journals and anthologies including *Sport Laureate, Typoetic, Drunk Monkeys, Spry, Biline*, and more. He is the author of *Elegy for a Star Girl (SWEP, 2017)* and three other collections of poetry. Grillo is a graduate of the University of New Haven where he played strong safety for the Chargers, and earned his MFA from Southern Connecticut State University. Grillo is an 11th grade English teacher in New Haven County, CT, where he lives with his wife Victoria (also an English teacher), their newborn son, Luciano, and their puppy-son, George. Visit the writer's website: https://www.christopheregrillo.com/

 twitter.com/cgrillo_writer

www.ingramcontent.com/pod-product-compliance
Lightning Source LLC
Chambersburg PA
CBHW021433070526
44577CB00001B/186